COW TALES

COW TALES

FOLKLORE FROM TEXAS AND THE AMERICAN SOUTHWEST

ELAINE KAVANAUGH JONES

SUNSTONE PRESS

SANTA FE

Sunstone books may be purchased for educational, business, or sales promotional use.
For information please write: Special Markets Department, Sunstone Press,
P.O. Box 2321, Santa Fe, New Mexico 87504-2321.

Book and cover design › Vicki Ahl
Body typeface › Palatino
Printed on acid-free paper
∞
eBook 978-1-61139-453-5

Library of Congress Cataloging-in-Publication Data

Names: Jones, Elaine Kavanaugh, 1952- author.
Title: Cowtales: folklore from Texas and the American southwest / by Elaine Kavanaugh
Jones.
Description: Santa Fe : Sunstone Press, [2016]
Identifiers: LCCN 2015048268 (print) | LCCN 2016010644 (ebook) | ISBN
9781632931122 (softcover : alk. paper) | ISBN 9781611394535 (ebook)
Subjects: LCSH: Texas--Folklore. | Southwestern States--Folklore.
Classification: LCC GR110.T5 J66 2016 (print) | LCC GR110.T5 (ebook) | DDC
398.209764--dc23
LC record available at http://lccn.loc.gov/2015048268

SUNSTONE PRESS IS COMMITTED TO MINIMIZING OUR ENVIRONMENTAL IMPACT ON THE PLANET.
THE PAPER USED IN THIS BOOK IS FROM RESPONSIBLY MANAGED FORESTS. OUR PRINTER HAS RECEIVED CHAIN OF CUSTODY
(COC) CERTIFICATION FROM: THE FOREST STEWARDSHIP COUNCIL™ (FSC®), PROGRAMME FOR THE ENDORSEMENT OF FOREST
CERTIFICATION™ (PEFC™), AND THE SUSTAINABLE FORESTRY INITIATIVE® (SFI®).
THE FSC® COUNCIL IS A NON-PROFIT ORGANIZATION, PROMOTING THE ENVIRONMENTALLY APPROPRIATE, SOCIALLY BENEFICIAL
AND ECONOMICALLY VIABLE MANAGEMENT OF THE WORLD'S FORESTS. FSC® CERTIFICATION IS RECOGNIZED INTERNATIONALLY
AS A RIGOROUS ENVIRONMENTAL AND SOCIAL STANDARD FOR RESPONSIBLE FOREST MANAGEMENT.

WWW.SUNSTONEPRESS.COM
SUNSTONE PRESS / POST OFFICE BOX 2321 / SANTA FE, NM 87504-2321 /USA
(505) 988-4418 / ORDERS ONLY (800) 243-5644 / FAX (505) 988-1025

THIS BOOK IS DEDICATED TO MY THREE ANGELS

Lillian
Maurine
Virginia

CONTENTS

I

THE WELL

Legend had it that the well never went dry even during the hottest drought of summer. Legend also had it that there was power in the water, almost magic. The old-timers covered it with a heavy, thick, solid round stone that took two mules to drop into place. Rain had become plentiful so the well was covered. Folks had put too much credit in that power. So what if the Henderson girl got over the fever and lived to a ripe old age after she bathed in it. So what if the Elderson's baby thrived after drinking it when the doctor said there was no way it would live. So what if Annie Fergerson's leg healed after her accident. A team of horses dragged her through a fence and the doctor said she'd never walk again. Her mother applied a water poultice and the leg healed.

I laughed at myself, half believing those old fables. But sure enough if it didn't rain soon we'd all be looking for the lost well. The lightning rod, liniment and windmill salesmen would be out of work. The whole state was in a drought, but this area was the worst. Streams, lakes and ponds that I had never seen dry before, were drying up. The river was only a trickle, almost stone dry.

I rode my horse out into the country where I'd heard the well was located. I was back to riding a horse since my car had been repossessed by the bank. I couldn't make the final payment. One payment left and I lost it all because of this thing called a Depression. Many people were out of work including me. But the President, Mr. Roosevelt, said over the radio, "better times were coming." Easy for him to say, he was rich. With a war looking close in Europe and every man begging even for food, how on God's earth could better times be coming?

I scouted the countryside but saw no sign of a well or giant stone. One thing for certain, it was the hottest driest time I could ever remember. My horse would give out soon, so I started back. Tomorrow, I'd try again.

For seven consecutive days, I went searching. I told no one, not even my wife, Lorena, who had a profile so beautiful that a man could go weak in the knees looking at her. Then I remembered someone saying old Mr. Lowrey, who'd gone blind, talked about the well. His daughter stationed him on a bench in front of the county store when she was too busy to watch him.

One morning, after several times of trying to catch him sitting there, I rode up to the store. Alas, there sat old man Lowrey. He was past ninety if he was a day. He had on faded worn overalls and an equally faded worn out shirt. His work boots had seen better days. They were tied with a string. He wore an old straw hat over his balding head. No matter that he was blind, his mind was sharp and his quick memory was sure to recollect exactly where that well was located.

I got off my horse, tied him to the hitching post. Then I walked over and sat down on the cane bottom chair next to the old man. Before I could utter a word, the old man burst out, "Don't tell me, I know who you are." We sat very quiet for a few minutes then the old man turned and smiled, "You're Totto, Annie and Lyman's boy. I bet you come to ask about the well."

Stunned, I said, "Yes sir, I have."

"I can't rightly tell you, but I can show you. I've still got my water witch stick somewhere if Jessie hadn't thrown it away. We'll have to go right about daylight so we won't die of heat stroke," the old man advised.

Again I sat stunned listening to the old man rambling away about the well. "You realize," he said, "that there well has healing properties. Some people around these parts didn't like that and insisted that it be capped. I was there when they rolled the stone over it. Took two mules and all their strength. You'll have to bring a wagon or a buggy. I can't ride a horse. Totto, you be at my place about daylight. I'll be waiting on the porch. Just cause I'm blind doesn't mean I can't think or hear. Being blind causes your hearing to be especially keen, like the eyes you don't have. Your other senses perk up sharper than before."

"But where was the well located? How are you going to direct me when you can't see?" I asked.

Laughing, the old man said, "You remember the old Grant mansion? I think it finally burned."

"Yes sir, it did," I told him.

"Are the gates still standing?" he asked. "They were ornate, very fine, and tall," he said.

"Been a long time since I was out that way. Was the well on their place?" I asked.

"Yes it was. That's partly why it was capped. They didn't like visitors coming all the time to get water, as if it was a shrine. A lot of hard times fell on the Grants when they closed that well. Remember, Totto?"

"Yes, come to think of it, I do. Their boy fell from the hay loft and broke his neck. Their daughter ran off with a man and never came back. Old man Grant had a stroke. His wife died taking care of him."

"You're right and if they'd just let it alone, that well could have done a lot of good," the old man insisted.

"You sure you can find it?" I asked.

"If you be at my place in the morning and drive me out there, I can find it. We'll have water for the whole dat gum community."

I sat silent, taking it all in carefully. The old man patted my shoulder. "Don't worry, Totto. I can see that water now. It was the clearest, cleanest most sparkling water that ever came from an underground spring. It never went dry." I rode home and got out my dusty old wagon stored in the barn. Never thought I would use it again. I wanted to make certain my horse could pull it. After some thought I knew it would take two horses to pull the wagon and carry two men.

I'd have to get Shady, my old work horse. My children called her Shady because she always headed for the shade every chance she got. At the end of the work day she raced for the big oak by the barn to rest in the shade. Nothing on God's earth could budge that horse from there until the next morning. I laughed as I called Shady out of the pasture.

The gauge in the barn read 113 degrees in the shade. There had to be a limit to how much heat people could bear. Tomorrow I'd take Mr. Arlo Winchester Lowrey out to find the well. There might just be a miracle waiting.

The next morning long before daylight, I hitched the horses to the wagon. An owl hooted from far off. I decided I'd better explain to Shady what we were going to do. Once we got out on the road, I began, "Now Shady, old girl, we're on a real important mission today. We are out to save the whole county. But I warn you, old girl, it's going to be hot today. No playing in the shade." With that, Shady snorted loudly. I thought I'd better quit talking before Shady stopped dead in her tracks.

Mr. Lowrey was waiting on the porch, just like he promised. No one else was in sight. There'd be no explaining to do.

By the time we rode out to the Grant property a blazing ball of sun was peeping over the trees. The old man was curiously silent. I didn't interrupt, both of us intent on our purpose. Sure enough the gate, the old man asked about, was there. It was tall, iron, and ornate. The gate was closed.

"Tell me what you see," the old man said.

"The gate, just like you described it" I told him.

"Once, I was in that house to a party. Prettiest stair case you ever saw, pure mahogany. But money don't matter. We know that now. Who is left of that family?"

"No one," I answered. No kin at all."

"Are the stone columns still standing, Toto?"

"Yes sir, all eight of them, charred by the fire." I answered.

"It was a hot night when the house burned. Fire wagons couldn't get out there till it was too late. Folks saw the flames for miles. It kind of spooked the place after that. But the well was spared. What we got to do is figure out where the back of the house ended cause the well was right outside the yard. Thing is, there was a rose bush that grew up right beside the well. The rose was a rambler, yellow with a glorious scent. Toto, if that rose is still there, growing among the weeds, you've as good as found the well," said the old man.

"I'll go walk it off. But was the house big?"

"Sure was, twenty eight rooms. It was the biggest house in this part of the county. Totto, when you locate that rose, come and get me. I want to be there when you find the well."

The sweat dripped off my face like rain drops and ran down my back. It puddled against my spine. It had to be 115 degrees in the shade. Before I could walk away, the old man called "Totto." I turned around to look at him. He appeared almost childlike. Not a drop of sweat was on his face. He wore old faded pants, thin as gauze, a white shirt, and red suspenders that held up his pants. Someone had attempted to sew the toe of one sock back together, tearing it even worse, as was evident since the toe of his shoe was worn through. I looked at his eyes. They were bright not dark, full of excitement.

"Yes sir." I answered.

"There's one more thing I haven't told you about the well," he said in a serious voice. "It won't do me no good to keep it to myself with no eyes to see it. So, I'm taking you into my confidence. You know, don't you, that Mr. Grant was a banker, owned the whole bank all by himself. There was a tale that people told after he died, that he hid some money in the well. It was said to be a great deal of money in an air tight red box. No one ever found it since the well was closed up."

The old man continued, "I was here when this well was dug, ninety nine feet deep. The Grants never had to worry about it drying up. It's forever water. They had water for washing, water for cattle, water for a garden and flowers. Mrs. Grant's roses were the talk of the town. The well was the best money could buy. It had brick walls and brass fixtures. Totto, somewhere in that well is thirty thousand dollars."

I couldn't take it all in or process it. I stood mute and stunned for all of ten minutes. " Totto, are you still there?" the old man called reaching out for me.

"Yes sir, I'm here. You've given me a mighty high assignment. But I'll do my best. You wait here. Don't wander off or you'll die in this heat," I warned the old man.

"Will do." He answered. "I'll stay right here."

With rivers of sweat blinding my eyes, I tried to put together all he'd told me. I walked away from the tall columns that had been a shaded porch. I tried to imagine the gigantic house and approximately how far it was to the rear of the house. Suddenly, a cardinal flew right past me toward the thicket and briars into the woods. That's when I saw the rose. It climbed high into a tree. Great yellow blossoms hung off its branches. I walked slowly toward the rose. When I reached it, I glanced down at the ground covered in old leaves, moss, fallen tree bark and sand. The heat was so intense that I wanted a drink of water more than anything. Then I saw something shiny, a brass ring in mortar. I dug through the briars and vines and there was the stone. It wasn't a a myth or a fable or a legend. The old man wasn't telling some wandering tale. Here it was: the well.

I traced my way back to the old man who sat waiting in the shade of the trees that were covered in vines and moss. I took his hand. It trembled.

"You found it," he said.

"Yep, only we have to get the stone off. Should I go for help?"

"No," he replied. "We can do it. The money, Totto, we have to see if the money is there. All these years, I've obsessed over it and now we're this close. Will you do it alone?"

"Yes sir, if I can." There was a rope in the wagon and I unhitched the horses fearing the worst, that Shady wouldn't move. I led them to the well. The old man held onto Shady's mane and stumbled along.

We finally made our way to the well. My heart was racing as I put the rope through the brass ring. The horses stood still as I tied the rope to their harnesses. It was as though they could sense our excitement. At first the rock wouldn't budge.

"It's been many a year that old stone lay there in the wind and weather. It's sealed shut with debris. Try again, Totto," the old man urged.

The horses made several false starts, then, stopped all together. I figured Shady would take a rest now. But she surprised me. Shady snorted loudly. She was ready to make one more try. The sound was like Easter morning when that stone was rolled away from the tomb. A loud cracking powerful pull and a sudden escape of air burst from the well. I could smell the water.

Before I could call out or move, the old man stepped forward and down he went, falling into the well.

Through shock and disbelief, I ran to the well's edge and fell on my knees. "Please God," escaped my lips.

"I ain't dead, Totto. Just doubled over, hung tight, wedged in the walls. Think my arm is broken," the old man shouted from the depths of the well.

"Thank you," I whispered. As I lifted my eyes, I saw a space, a sort of compartment in the brick walls. There was no time to lose treasure hunting. "Hold on, I'll get you out," I shouted loudly above ground.

I lowered the rope into the well. "If you can put this rope around your waist or under your arms, I'll hoist you up with the horses," I shouted.

"Don't think I can do that, not the way I'm turned." The old man's voice sounded weakly from the well.

"Let me think. I'll have to go for help."

"Nope, don't do that. Everyone would know what an old fool I am. Climb down in here, Totto."

"We might both go down then." I said.

"Don't think so. These walls are solid. Maybe we can figure out where the money is."

I climbed carefully into the well, knowing exactly the hiding place of the money, If I could put the rope around the old man, I could get him out.

"Are you in pain?" I asked the old man once I hovered above him in the well. My feet were planted firmly against the sides of the well.

"Not yet. I'm just kind of stunned," he said in a weak voice.

"I'll have you out in a bit." Once I slipped the rope around him, I climbed back out of the well and put the rope through the horses' harness. I'd have to keep them steady and not let them spook. "You ready down there," I said with great anguish.

"Let her go, Totto!"

It was a welcome sight when the old man came tumbling out of the well. Propping his good arm over my shoulder we pulled him to his feet. He was bruised, battered, and had a broken arm.

"Got a surprise for you," I told him. Being careful not to drop the red box, I reached down into the compartment in the side of the wall. I quickly found the box and lifted it out. The old man's face lit up like a Christmas tree when I placed it in his good hand.

"Quick open it, hurry!" he shouted with excitement.

I worked the latch of the engraved box and my eyes gazed at the contents.

"What's in it? Tell me what do you see? Totto."

"The money, sure enough," I exclaimed.

"Count it. Tell me how much is there," the old man said.

Carefully, I lifted the first bill and it wasn't even damp. The box was air tight. "How long ago did Mr. Grant die?" I asked.

"More than ten years," the old man replied.

"The money is here, perfectly safe. Only there's a problem."

"What's that?" the old man asked.

"The bills are all one thousand dollar bills."

"Lord, have mercy. Can't even cash it at no bank around here in these hard times or we'll be accused of robbery. Wish my old blind eyes could see it. We'll have to study on this, Totto. There's one other thing. Will you get me a drink from the well?" the old man asked.

"Don't know how I'd get the water. Don't even have a bucket." I replied.

"Once there was a barn. Guess it's gone too," the old man said.

"I'll find out," I said as I started to look for the barn. From a distance, the barn was colossal. Lightning rods with glass ornaments, things of great beauty sparkled in the sun. Who except the very wealthy could afford such extravagance? I quickened my step excitedly. What looked so intact from a distance was a ruin close up. The building was as big as an opera house or hotel.

Storage areas for wagons were directly inside. Steps led into rooms and a wide staircase was to the left. I raced up the stairs two at a time. Before me was a hay loft large enough to hold thousands of bales. But the roof was mostly gone; a crow could fly through. I knew better than to chance taking another step. There'd be no one to rescue me. I sadly went back down the staircase, understanding the fascination the old man had for the place. But he'd known it in bygone days at the height of its glory.

Then I saw a door straight ahead of me, a door of pure mahogany. An eerie chill ran down my spine. I'd been gone a long while. I slammed myself against the door. It creaked open. Inside was an office. A huge desk, cluttered and dust covered sat in the center of the room. A crystal gas lamp hung overhead. One window looked out over the countryside. Cob webs hung from the ceiling.

Who could ever have lived in such wealth when the rest of us were so poor? But Mr. Grant was a banker. Money was nothing to him. He touched it, counted it, and trusted it every day of his life.

My eyes caught sight of a rusty safe. I crouched down and touched the lock. With no combination, I could never open it. I turned the knob and it opened. Inside, were two crystal glasses, a bottle of liquor and a tarnished silver bucket, nothing else.

As I carried the treasure out, I saw a painting on a shadowy wall. The painting had a gilt-frame surrounding a scene of a gate at the edge of some green woods. There were pink clouds above the gate and a flock of white dove flying overhead.

Back at the well, I lowered the tarnished bucket into its depths and heard a splash.

"You were gone so long I nearly went into a panic," the old man said.

I poured water into the crystal glass.

"Better than champagne."He smiled as he drank.

"You never tasted champagne in your life," I said to him.

"Sure did, right here at a party, when I was twenty. This place was so alive, like a town unto itself." He took another sip of the exceptionally clear, clean, sparkling water.

On the trip back to town we both were silent, taking into account what had happened. The doctor put a plaster cast and sling on the old man's arm. I drove him home.

The next morning I rode out with the town officials to show them the well. All the town folk took wagons and went for water. Families had gone without water because of this terrible drought. Busy as I was, I didn't see the old man for days.

His daughter turned up pleading, "It's Daddy. He's calling for you, Totto. He's got pneumonia."

When I reached the old man's bedside, I saw that his eyes were strangely alight. "You had to be the first to know," he said.

"To know what?" I asked.

"Thank you, Totto, for giving me a sure enough adventure. Look at me. I can see! It's the water from the well I drank that did it. Now I can see my Lord and Savior when I get to heaven."

"Slow down. What do you mean?" I asked.

The old man smiled a mysterious smile. He looked directly into my eyes. A moment later, Mr. Arlo Winchester Lowery was gone. He left everything else to me.

2

The Hundred Year Old Cow

We called her, The Hundred Year Old Cow. She was past thirty five years because she'd been a young heifer when Grand Daddy was alive. Now she was all jutting bones with every rib, both hips and pelvis showing through. She could barely walk anymore, but she loved to graze. All summer, I'd seen her happily munching away on the range land with the other cows.

Come first frost and first bad cold spell, she got down and couldn't get up. I raced to town and bought four bags of sweet mash. I came back and poured a circle of it around her. She ate her way through it, pushed and shoved and got up. Trouble was, after that, she was hooked on sweet mash.

So we fed her every day. Those were her golden days. She'd had thirty plus calves and only last spring she had a bull calf. If she could have talked, she could have told some tales, about the winters, standing in the snow and rain, and how sweet spring smelled when it finally came She'd probably tell about coyotes roaming around the herd, and bob cats, when she was still a young heifer.

The Hundred Year Old Cow got so spoiled that she'd stand and wait for us to bring her bucket of mash every morning. She'd turn her head as we drove down in the pickup truck and gaze with her big brown eyes. I'd swear that she was smiling. She had horns and probably in her young days she could be fierce, protecting her calf or pushing some other cow away from the hay. She could still use those horns to her advantage. Gradually I won her trust. Then when I fed her, she'd gently lay her head against my shoulder. At first, it frightened me, but I realized she was thanking me.

As the drought worsened, it was a real struggle for her to walk to the water trough. Turning her poor crippled body and carrying the enormous frame must have painful beyond our understanding.

She became a familiar figure and much loved. Even the grandchildren would say "Let's go feed The Hundred Year Old Cow."

Then one morning she wasn't there with the herd. We looked and looked everywhere, but she'd simply vanished. I walked the woods for hours searching. The other cows finally got my attention. They were running back and forth across a ravine. It had rained a few days before, breaking the drought. I walked slowly into the ravine, fearful of what I might find.

There she was, bogged up to her neck, covered in mud, even her face and horns. I went across the mud to her. I found she was alert, though she was slowly suffocating. I felt a lump in my throat so big I couldn't do anything except touch her face. She looked at me and chewed. I knew what I had to do, but there was one thing first.

I brought her one last bucket of sweet mash. She happily ate it, seemingly unaware of her fate.

I walked to the barn and told my brother that I'd found her. He determined that her hip was broken and to try and pull her out of the mud would hurt her more.

"She'd never get up", my brother said. I watched helpless as he took out his rifle.

"Wait," I said. "I've got to tell her goodbye." I crossed the mud and looked into her brown eyes, "Remember, we love you and we won't ever forget you", I told her.

My brother waited till I got back to the pickup. I heard the shot that ended the life of The Hundred Year Old Cow.

The strangest thing happened. The whole herd suddenly came running right up to me. They stopped short. One red cow that I'd fed during a sick spell, came forward and walked slowly to me. Her eyes looked straight into mine.

"What are they doing?" I asked my brother.

"They're thanking you," he answered.

3

THE COWBOY

Above him the stars blazed more brightly than any city lights, unhindered by competition. He shivered slightly even though it was June and the camp fire burned high. He knew his time was running out, but he still hadn't decided what to do. All the boys had high-tailed it to town. He told them he could manage the herd alone. It was a two hour ride to the ranch and nearly that long to town for supplies. They had left him alone for five days and nights. There was nothing much to do, watch the cows, hunt stragglers, and check for new calves.

The first two days and nights went smoothly, no problems. He could hear coyotes howling far off. He took his horse and rode the herd, but could see nothing out of the ordinary. The third day ten young heifers had their calves. One had a little trouble but he helped her and she did fine.

Wild flowers brightened the whole countryside with moon yellow, scarlet, royal blue and pure white. The boys would laugh at him for appreciating flowers. They cared about good beer, fast women and dependable horses.

This life had suited him. There was a good deal of alone time. He'd come to this job by chance. His parents both died young. His mom died from breast cancer at age 39 and his dad suddenly died from a heart attack at age 41. The death of both his parents had left him alone. Before settling their estate, he finished college.

The only girl he ever cared about betrayed him. He took her to a dance and caught her in the arms of his best friend. He could see her long blonde hair as she drew back when they were caught. Her beautiful face was pale as the moon, her lips bright pink. After that, he never trusted life again. She begged him to come back, but his heart was broken and he'd never forget the memory of her and his best buddy standing in the dark together.

He settled his parent's estate. The last night at their pretty little homestead he spent wrapping his mother's glassware. He grabbed another piece of newspaper, an ad caught his eye. It read: Wrangler wanted, good pay, long hours, fine rewards.

It sounded just right to him, being raised on a farm. He put the money from the sale in the bank and took a train south. He'd always rode a horse, worked cattle and the last few years had no ties to bind him so the job suited him well, except for the aloneness. Sometimes at night, he woke to go sit by the campfire till the memory of her beautiful face faded. Maybe she really meant what she told him. Maybe he'd acted in haste. Maybe after his parents both went so suddenly, his grief hadn't allowed his heart to heal enough to forgive her. He'd never know now.

He stuffed a piece of paper in his pocket that would let her know he had forgiven her. There was a bag of Indian arrowheads too, that he'd found. He'd spent a lot of time walking the territory where they herded the cows. Once he'd found a whole cache of arrowheads while out riding. He stopped near a creek and on a rocky outcropping he'd paused and looked down. Scattered on the ground were twenty or so perfect artifacts. He marveled at the workmanship of the flints. He found arrows, knives, and a few tiny bird points. The bird points were his favorites. He guessed some Indian had lost them there or hidden them and never returned for them. The note in his shirt pocket asked the boys to pass them on to her. Maybe she'd have a son someday who'd cherish them like he did.

He didn't know why the boys hadn't made it back on the fifth day, but he guessed that's why everything happened the way it did. In his note he told them to never leave a solitary man to guard camp and summer cattle again.

A freak rain storm came in out of nowhere suddenly the day before. Dark clouds hovered overhead with fierce fingers of lightning, hard winds, cracking and rumbling so loud the cows spooked. He regretted that two baby calves were trampled and one young heifer had her hip broken and he had to shoot her. But later, soaking wet by the campfire, he finally settled down near his dog. The cows were gentle now after all their running and bellowing. He fell asleep, dead asleep. Startled, he woke up to the yellow eyes of a coyote looking down on him. Its mouth was curled in a snarl with foam dripping from his jaws. It attacked him.

They struggled until he finally reached his knife in his belt. He must have stabbed that coyote fifty times before it fell off of him. His face was bitten and clawed the worst. His arms were also torn. How it got him so bad he couldn't figure. He was in shock and pain.

The coyote was mangy, had sores and fleas, and he knew for certain it was rabid. Now he was in for it. He remembered the look on his mother's face when the doctor told her that she had breast cancer. After the surgery, she looked at him and his dad said, "I can't live like this. I can't ever love life again."

His dad couldn't live without her. Less than a year later, he was gone too.

It seemed like life was stacked against him. Now this had happened to him. He knew exactly how his mother had felt.

The boys found him the next day near the campfire. His dog was still guarding him. His face showed clearly the marks of his recent encounter with the coyote. His rifle had fallen to his side.

"We had to shoot a cow once that went mad," one of the cowboys said. "It wasn't a pretty sight, something about the nervous system that rabies affects."

"Yea, and don't forget that old dog that wandered onto the ranch that time," the other cowboy reminded him.

They found the note in his shirt pocket. Parts of it brought tears to their eyes as they read it over his grave when they buried him.

"He sure loved that girl," they all agreed.

They tied a blue silk scarf on the small cross they built, figuring it must have been hers since he died holding it in his hand.

4

STUCK

Last night I dreamed that I heard my little dog, Routy, barking. Far off in the distance my old cow, Belinda, was bellowing. When I reached for my wife the bed was empty. I woke with trembling and shock to remember that they were all gone years ago. I lay in the moonlight trying hard to collect my addled wits.

My wife passed away two years ago after discovering she had breast cancer. Neither she nor I could deal with the consequences of the disease. She was gone before either of us accepted the diagnosis. The loss of her was unbearable. It was not only the loss of a wife, but a friend, companion and soul mate. We'd shared common ground, married young (she was seventeen; I was eighteen). Both of us were from strict farm families. We'd bought a farm and made a go of it, living well. We'd run a couple of hundred cows and raised crops.

Our only child, Andy died in a car crash just after attending the Senior Prom. He was the perfect son, straight A's in school, football hero, about to accept a scholarship to veterinary school. I'd bought him a new truck. He died in that truck. Shortly after, my wife came home to find a small brown and white dog sitting on our back steps. We named him, Routy. That dog lived fifteen years.

Our son, Andy had come late in life when we'd given up any hope of having children. My wife was thirty-nine when Andy was born. Fortunately Routy outlived her. She was spared that grief.

Belinda was a whole different story. She always seemed like an old cow. She was my wife's favorite. Belinda looked as long as a train. She was a nice umber color, almost topaz. Her face wasn't ugly, but it wasn't pretty either because of her fierce expression. Her perfectly shaped extra-long horns could be used as a weapon if necessary. Her most redeeming feature was golden blond bangs that looked as if she combed them every day. Each morning she'd follow my wife around waiting for table scraps. In summer, her favorite treat was watermelon. How that cow loved watermelon.

Even though Belinda stopped having calves, my wife kept loving her. Belinda became a herd cow. With her distinctive bellow, she could make the cows do anything. Belinda could turn them on a dime, even in a stampede.

My wife's last words through the delirium of the morphine were in loving regard to Belinda. "Daddy, is it sale day? Don't you be selling Belinda! You know how I love her. Promise me, Daddy." Sitting in silence, I could only nod and pat her hand.

Just before sunrise, on what promised to be the hottest day of summer, I stepped out on the porch, coffee in hand. It was the only time there was any cool since we were living in the worst drought for over fifty years. I was glad my wife wasn't here to see how I'd let the yard go. Every rose bloomed because of the way she had always carefully tended the. The St. Augustine grass was pale to the roots. But most of all, I noticed Belinda was nowhere in sight.

Maybe she'd given up on my wife coming out with scraps and watermelon, but she still looked for her. Or maybe she'd just wondered off to graze. When she didn't return by nine o'clock, I figured I'd better saddle up. I owed it to my darling, Annie, to see after Belinda especially since I'd neglected everything else.

At the only stock pond with any water remaining, I found Belinda. To my absolute astonishment, she was having a calf. Yes, the Lord works in mysterious ways. Belinda was up to her hips in mud. Her calf, born minutes earlier, sprawled on the mud. If Belinda weren't the only cow around, I'd swear the calf wasn't hers. She had to be nearly twenty-five years old. "How'd you manage this, Belinda? Wonders never cease, "I called to her."

About that time, she lunged at me with her horns and sunk deeper in the mud. Her calf let out a pitiful wail. I knew I was in trouble. Seventy-three year old men don't pull twenty-five hundred pound cows out of the worst mud hole in Texas much less, Belinda. The sun was about to become broiling hot. I'd come off from home without rope or chain of any kind whatsoever to help a distressed animal. The only coverage affording Belinda and her calf was a tall magnificent cottonwood tree near the bank of the dried up pond.

Most people don't understand a drought. In times of normal rain fall, river flow, creeks run, stock ponds fill up. Animals have to walk long distances to find water in a drought. Bird must fly out of their domain to water. Cows that have watered at the same place for ten, fifteen years go there to find water and it's dry. I guess that's what Belinda did. In her memory, water was plentiful at the stock ponds. Animals never reason like humans. No wonder she went ill-tempered on me for joking. Belinda was in a nasty predicament.

"I'm going for a rope. I'll be back," I told Belinda.

She snorted and tried to move, but no chance. She was stuck tight.

When I reached the barn, I found my best rope, got a better saddle and exchanged my cap for a wide-brimmed hat. Back at the stock pond, after considerable snorting and trying to drive a horn through me, Belinda settled down. She let me put a rope on her horns. The calf looked as if time was running out for him.

As much as I tried, nothing would budge Belinda. She was getting mighty testy the more I yanked on her. A clear mental picture came to me then. My small John Deer tractor sat under the garden shed. Better yet, there were ten to twelve watermelons in the garden patch.

I tried to explain to Belinda what I was going to do, but she gave me one of her fierce looks. The calf was trying to move closer to Belinda. Only she was buried so deep in the mud that it was impossible.

"I won't fail you, Annie," I said out loud," or Belinda either."

By the time I aired up a low tire and put another battery on the John Deere, it was nearly noon. The wind blew like a furnace. I went to the house and downed two bottle of water.

Back at the stock pond, Belinda stood waiting none too happy for my slowness. She perked up upon seeing the tractor, and the couple of watermelons I'd brought along to entice her. I walked across the mud carefully to put the rope on Belinda's horns when she lunged at me. In seconds, I was sunk as deep as Belinda in the mud, wondering if it was quicksand. Belinda gave me a look of pure disgust and turned her head away to snort.

We were there in the mud with the tractor roaring when I heard thunder. Thinking it must be the affect of the heat. I was stunned when angry dark clouds moved rapidly over us. The weather report that morning stated clearly no rain was in the forecast for at least ten day.

The first raindrop hit me square between the eyes, hard as a slap. A gust of wind blew my hat off. The thunder was right over us, deafening. The calf bawled loudly. I looked at Belinda and she looked at me. Suddenly a thunder clap sounded, shaking the ground as hard as an earthquake. Heavy rain so thick that I could barely see Belinda pelted us like buck shot. I knew I'd better do something before Belinda decided to use her horns as a weapon.

I pulled hard on the ropes only moving myself a fraction. The movement threw the tractor in gear. I came out of that mud like greased lightening. The tractor stalled after rolling into the cottonwood tree. I looked back at the stock pond to the most amazing sight of my life.

Belinda lifted her back leg out of the mud with a great sucking noise, then pulling herself up, tugging against the mud until she made it to the shore. Her calf followed meekly, bawling loudly.

Belinda looked at me as if to say, "Couldn't wait all day for you to get me out of here."

She and her calf followed me home walking behind the tractor. I put them in the barn, scattered hay for the calf and watermelons for Belinda. At the house, I peeled off my muddy, soaking wet clothes heading for the shower.

"Well, Annie," I said loudly, "I don't know which one of us rescued the other, but Belinda is safely home. And Annie, you'll never believe this. Belinda has a calf."

It rained for four consecutive days and nights. Every stock pond was filled. Every creek ran. The river flowed at full capacity. Belinda never had another calf. She raised Little Belinda gracefully, injecting as much personality into her as possible. One day when Little Belinda was getting ready to have her first calf, I found Belinda down under her favorite tree. I took her some watermelon. She refused.

I sat with her all night. Her breathing was labored like Annie's had been, just before she died. Sometime near dawn, I fell asleep. Belinda did too.

She's still resting under that tree. A great iron cross marks the place. That cow was as dear to me as Annie, as Andy, and as Routy.

As for Little Belinda, she wasn't as fond of watermelon as her mother. But her calf, let me put it this way. I've added seven more acres to my watermelon patch.

5

ODE TO A WEDDING

As he regained consciousness he slowly opened his eyes. Gradually he became aware of the sound of flapping wings. Surely he hadn't died and gone to heaven. No, that was too easy. As he opened his eyes wincing at the sharp aching pain in his leg, the sight that greeted him was so startling and horrifying, he almost wished that he had died and gone to heaven.

Buzzards. Hundreds and hundreds of them were circling overhead. He'd never seen so many buzzards in his life. Many were on the ground, a half mile away. In his unconsciousness he'd been dreaming that it was snowing and Christmas time. Now, he knew that it wasn't snow at all, but the dust the buzzards were kicking up, doing their buzzard dance. Something was lying on the ground halfway across the field. He saw his horse horribly twisted lying dead.

They'd come to search for an old cow who didn't return with the herd. She was thirty years old which was rare for a cow. Her trouble was that she was just too stubborn to die. That skinny Hereford had huge horns that framed her bald face. He called her the Old Lady. Now his horse had stepped in an armadillo hole and broken its neck. He had been thrown and lay with his leg broken. He was on foot, ten miles from home and almost helpless. His leg began to throb. At least the bone wasn't sticking through the flesh. He'd figure out what to do.

Those buzzards were closing in and the next target was him. One swooped awkwardly at him. He ducked and swung his arm in the air. He didn't have long until he became a buzzard feast. He stood; his leg hurt the worst of any pain he'd ever known. He had to stand or else he'd be the next meal of these overhead circling hungry birds. He'd seen a man once who lost an eye that had been picked out by a vulture while he was stranded on a mesa herding sheep. He silently gave thanks that he wasn't in the desert.

A tree limb lay a few feet away. He managed to crawl over and grab it, then stand. Walking would be something else entirely. A buzzard landed on his poor dead horse. He waved his arms wildly to chase it away. He had to find his rifle and figure out how to get back to the ranch. He decided to drag his saddle away. He'd have to come back for it later. No time for tears over the memories of his beloved horse. But the memories stabbed at him anyway. He couldn't help but remember riding in the town's Fourth of July parade, and going to the saloon on Saturday night. That horse always brought him home when he was too drunk to know where he was.

After his visits to the saloon his mother made him go to church for three consecutive Sundays. That turned out to be a blessing because that's where he met Bessie Wilsap. They'd gone riding together for a year. She was the most beautiful girl he ever saw. Bessie had blonde hair, eyes so blue that the whole sky could get lost in them and white even teeth so straight that he could think of nothing else, except running his tongue over them. Bessie was young, sweet, ambitious. He had really liked her, but it didn't work out.

Folks said she went off to some ladies college up north and studied medicine. He'd never forget her. Yep, he should have given her the ring before he kissed her. "Well Bessie, I bet you never forgot that kiss especially since you made me stand two feet from you to deliver it," he shouted out loud to the wind and the buzzards. "I've still got that ring. It's diamonds with sapphires like your eyes". And this is where a kiss like that lands you, all alone, miles from home with a broken leg and no help in sight.

A buzzard swooped so low that it nearly knocked him down. He ducked the creature and reached for his hat that was mashed under the bridle of his horse. The woods looked far away, but they were his destination. He just wanted to be any where from this endless sea of buzzards.

Leaning hard on the tree limb, he limped, dragged, complained and cussed all the way to where the majority of the buzzards were congregating. He saw finally what brought them to this spot. It was the afterbirth of a calf. What cow could have been here, he wondered. Only the Old Lady was missing but thirty year old cows don't have calves.

It took him the best part of the day to reach the woods with all his stops to rest. By the time he crossed to the other side he was so exhausted he could only think of one thing: sleep. He lay with his back against a tree and slept. When he woke up it was sundown and he was hungry. He heard the unmistakable sound of bellowing. Out of the bush and briars came the Old Lady. Trailing directly behind her was the tiniest calf he'd ever seen. If the Old Lady hadn't been alone, he'd been one hundred percent positive that it wasn't her calf. But considering the facts, he had no choice but to accept the calf as hers.

"I'd never have thought it possible," he said to the old Lady. "You're full of surprises." The Old Lady bellowed and the tiny calf made a sound somewhere between that of a lamb or goat, but nothing like a calf.

Then a golden thought came to him. A thought so intelligent that he smiled about the biggest grin he'd ever smiled.

When daylight came, he had spent the night trying to reach home by the only means available. His leg was swollen tight in his boot. He crossed a creek and came upon a country road so familiar to him. The sun had started to climb over the horizon when suddenly a buggy and horse came rumbling down the road. He had no time to make a move. The buggy approached him and the woman driving it pulled up and stopped.

"Grisham Graham Ingleholt, what on earth are you doing riding a cow this time of the morning? Don't tell me. Another late night in town? Guess you really tied one on. Where's your horse?" the woman asked.

Exhaustion, fever, pain and shock now took hold of him he felt himself passing out. The next thing he knew some awful smelling salts were passed back and forth under his nose. The face of Bessie Wilsap hovered above. "Your leg is broken, Grisham. What on earth happened? Don't worry, I'll get you in the buggy and we'll tie this poor old cow to the back."

The next thing he knew he was lying in a soft bed. His leg in a plaster cast, was propped on a pillow. The Old Lady was bellowing outside the window and Bessie Wilsap was standing in the doorway of the room.

"Can you talk now, Grisham?" He'd been humiliated to the tenth degree and now the woman who'd jilted him wanted answers. She came closer. "Should I go contact your mother," Bessie asked.

Without thinking he answered, "Ma passed away two years ago."

"I'm sorry, Grisham, I didn't know," Bessie said with sincerity.

"Why did you leave, Bessie?" he asked next.

"Because Grisham, nothing was going to stop me from being a doctor, not a man or love or anything. Certainly not you because I'd already lost my heart and if I stayed, I'd lose my chance at a career too. Besides you had a lot of wild oats to sew back then."

"Well Bessie, those oats done been sewn and burned up in the hot sun." he said bitterly.

She came close to his bed. "I'm sorry, Grisham. I cared too much about you to stay. I've wanted to be a doctor all my life, not just somebody's wife."

He was silent and glanced out the window. The Old Lady and her calf stood by a tree. The calf was nursing heartily.

"Look Grisham, I have more patients to see after. You rest and I'll be back before dark."

He looked at her attentively. Her beauty hadn't faded at all. "Guess I should thank you for..."

"Don't talk, just rest I'll be back later." Bessie said as she tied her bonnet and picked up a black bag. Later in the day, just as she promised, Bessie returned and came to his room with a steaming bowl of chicken broth.

"Are you feeling better?" she asked. "Are you ready to tell me what happened to cause you to ride that poor old cow home.

He began to tell her about his horse, how the Old Lady had been missing and those demon buzzards. When he spoke about his horse, Bessie actually had tears in her eyes, showing a concern that comes only from true love.

"Oh Grisham, I'm sorry you've been through so much. You lay right there and recover," Bessie ordered.

Only he'd had about had enough bossing. After all, he'd been on his own for a long time. He threw back the covers, pulled his leg over the side of the bed, and tried to stand. The room began to spin and down he went, stricken, ashamed and humiliated.

Bessie ran to his side and helped him back to bed. The mere closeness of her, her scent and those sapphire eyes, stirred the love he had for her in his heart. Her tender arms held him and he leaned toward her.

"Don't you dare, Grisham Graham Ingleholt. Don't you dare kiss me."

"Are you going to make me give you an engagement ring first, or stand two feet away?" he asked defensively.

"I'm going to make you lie down and get better before we talk about marriage."

"Marriage," he said.

"Certainly. Engagement Rings and kisses of fire. I'm not a dance hall girl, I'm a fully qualified doctor, respected here about," Bessie said with the confident conviction only educated folk have.

"I haven't been around dance hall girls since you left," he said.

Bessie smiled. "I'm happy to know that, Grisham. I'm also happy you care enough about an old cow to go hunting for her and risk everything. Shows a fair amount of character."

Six weeks later, at the Presbyterian Church with the biggest crowd ever gathered on Christmas Eve, Doctor Bessie Wilsap and Grisham Graham Ingleholt tied the knot.

More than one cowboy was heard saying, "I never thought I'd see the day when Gris would be marrying in a church. Wonder why that cow is here?"

Bessie's cousin of almost equal beauty, was maid of honor, and caught the wedding bouquet. She said, "Isn't Bessie the most beautiful bride?" to a nodding crowd.

Just as they ran out of the church amid rice, distant Christmas carols and felicitations, some one announced "It's snowing." Then, "Why's that cow here?"

The Old Lady and her calf were stationed by the hitching post. With snow covering her skinny red back she bellowed. Her tiny calf let out a bleat, somewhere between a sheep and a goat. After all, if it wasn't for the Old Lady, there wouldn't have been a wedding today.

Hallelujah! Amen!

6

MYSTERY AT ADOBE CANYON

The storm warnings spoke of high wind, ice, snow, and plummeting temperatures. But the radio forecast specifically stated that the storm wouldn't arrive until afternoon.

When my Dad's cow hands brought in the herd nearly intact, except for a few stragglers, our foreman and I decided to go round up the rest before the storm hit. We'd ridden out five or six miles and saw tracks where cattle headed up river toward a canyon many miles farther. We continued after them, figured we'd capture them and be back at the ranch before the storm.

When we reached the canyon, one of the heifers was trying to have her calf. By the time we'd helped her with the birth, the foreman pointed toward the northwest. Never before or since have I witnessed such a sight. The sky was dark as night, edged with pink and the predicted storm was moving toward us with frightening velocity. Onward it came swallowing up every inch of the sky. Lightning flashed all around. There was a strange eerie silence. "We'd best ride like the wind into that canyon ahead and find some cover," the foreman said with surprising calm.

The cattle, already sensing what was to come, were galloping in a straight line, even the newborn calf, moving at a trot behind its mother. We weren't prepared to wait out a storm. At least we had on our winter coats. Our saddles were loaded with a rolled blanket, canteen, a rope, little else except maybe some jerky.

Within twenty minutes, the snow began; at first only fluff, then in earnest, heavy wet snow, brutal cold. The cattle had denned up in a steep-walled overhang almost a cave. The foreman and I joined them with our horses.

"How long do you think we will be here?" I asked.

"A while," he answered, always a man of few words.

He was right. By late afternoon, it was darker than midnight and we had already gathered kindling, started a fire, and hovered close simply to keep warm. As I walked deeper into the canyon in search of wood, I saw ruins of adobe walls. In the light of the cedar limb torch I carried, they produced a haunting that followed me back to the camp. "There's ruins farther down the canyon," I told the foreman.

"The old ones, the ancients, Indians," he replied, his face lined over the fire.

"Are there arrow heads?"

"Arrow heads, pots, grain, sandals," he replied.

"Sandals?" I asked.

"Sandals," he repeated. "I've been here before, Boy. It's best leave it all alone. The storm will pass and we'll get out of here. At least these walls and the precipice give us shelter," he said, offering me some jerky.

The cows huddled close for warmth. The new born calf bawled loudly, moved close to its mother then nursed.

"How do you know these things?" I asked the foreman, always curious about him because he never talked much, but his abilities were grand enough that my Dad made him foreman.

"I worked these parts as a young man, knew this country like a map; my wife and son were with me then."

"What happened to them that you're all alone now?" I asked.

"They're gone," he answered. "Let's build up the fire. We're going to be here for the night."

Once we had the fire blazing we hovered close with our blankets around us for it was bitter cold. I studied the foreman's face. Clearly, he had been handsome. He still had the finest set of teeth I'd ever seen, perfect, straight, white as summer bright. His eyes were brilliant blue, starlit. As I watched the snow fall on his dark blonde hair with hardly a silver strand, I wondered fiercely at the bits and fragments of the story he'd told me. All night the snow fell in showers of great flakes like pure white feathers from angel wings. By the fireside, our foreman continued to add wood telling me gently, "Sleep, Boy."

Sometime during the night I woke to find the fire died down to orange red embers. Our foreman was asleep. My movement jerked him awake and he reached for his gun. "I was only going to get more wood," I explained.

The snow was still falling thickly, rich, white, and wet. The whole countryside appeared illuminated. Our horses huddled under the precipice. The cattle stood silently sleeping. The foreman, now fully awake, carefully laid some timbers on the fire. Immediately they began to pop, rack loudly and send out cinders like fireworks.

"We aren't burning Indian timber, are we?" I asked.

"No, but some of the cowboys found firewood still lying ready by the pits as if the Indians departed suddenly and never returned."

"Wonder why?" I asked.

"They may have been under attack and it wasn't safe to come home, if they escaped at all. Or maybe they went hunting and were captured," our foreman answered. "They left in haste, that's for certain."

Sensing that he had warmed up to me, I took a chance. "What happened to your wife and child?" I asked.

The foreman stared into the fire a long while in silence. I feared he wouldn't answer. "They died in an accident. The boy would be older than you, a man. If only I'd warned them. If only I'd been more careful. My young wife didn't know cattle or ranches, wild animals or danger. She was a proper lady. To her, riding was a hobby, not a job. She was barely twenty when she died. I should never have brought her here."

"You can't blame yourself, you musn't."

"Boy, you're too young to understand. They've been gone close to thirty years. There's never a moment they aren't on my mind. The fire is going good, you'd best sleep. Looks doubtful we'll get out of here in the morning. I sure hope you like jerky."

My heart was deeply touched by this man whom I'd never heard speak hardly at all. The idea of him sharing a secret so painful gave me a most tender feeling, as if he was my relative or my Dad. When morning came, it was cold as Christmas with snow drifts ten feet high. The snow continued to fall. Gray heavy clouds threatened more.

"We're in luck, Boy. I found a little pan and some coffee in my saddle bag. I'll melt some snow and boil us a cup. You go gather some more wood for us if you don't mind."

"What about the cattle? What will they eat?" I asked.

"The old ones left so quickly, their corn was found in the ruins, stored in giant pottery jars. So maybe you'll find some."

The wind had blown snow so high that walking was difficult. The cold numbed my hands and feet as soon as I left the fireside. Only I was glad to return to the ruins, thankful that our foreman had given me an excuse.

The snow made terraces and walls a ghostly mauve splendor. I almost expected people to appear from the doorways and windows. I climbed upward toward a stone wall onto a platform. Not another step did I take. My feet slipped from under me. Down I went, my body falling hard, pitched against a stone floor. In the cold empty blackness, my twelve year old heart sank in trembling fear. My eyes searched the darkness. Gradually, I saw light high above in an opening. I began to pray loudly for the foreman to come and rescue me.

It seemed hours before he came shouting and calling, "Boy, where are you? Answer me, Boy. Can you hear me?"

Tears welled in my eyes. My throat went so dry that only a gasp came out. The foreman must have been terrified that I was lost forever like his wife and son.

"Here," I croaked. "I'm down here," I called, listening to the echo.

"You've fallen in one of the Old Ones' kivas. Thank God it's winter. Fer-de-lance."

"Fer-de-lance. What's that?" I asked.

"Lethal snakes, but tropical. Out here, there are only rattlers. But I've known them to den up in a kiva. I used to snake hunt. They could be heard rattling in those old ruins down in a kiva. I'll get my rope and horse. We'll pull you out. Don't worry," the relief sounding in his voice.

Just as the foreman pulled me from the kiva, the sky opened up and a shaft of light pierced through the clouds so brilliant that we had to shield our eyes. The snow slacked to a dusting. That's when I saw it, a scattering of Indian arrowheads fallen from a woven quiver. In a hasty escape, someone had dropped this treasure, decades ago.

The foreman was busy stringing up his rope on his saddle. My mind became frantic trying to figure out how to claim the arrowheads. My desperation was so intense that I began to sweat in the freezing cold. I knew I could not leave them behind no matter that the foreman specifically told me not to take anything from the ruins.

"Come on, Boy, let's go back to camp. If the sun comes out, we'll be able to leave this afternoon. The snow has stopped. "Hey, what's this?" He called. Suddenly, I heard the crack of a falling wall. A giant clay pot shattered, spilling corn everywhere.

"Old corn is better than nothing," our foreman remarked, holding dark yellow kernels in his hand. "Help me gather it."

I began to put the corn in my hat, knowing full well it would take several trips to get enough. I never glanced back too fearful I'd betray myself.

On my last trip to the ruins, while the foreman brewed our coffee, I claimed the treasure trove of arrowheads. Their beauty glistened like gold. Mine for the taking. I quickly stashed them in my saddle bag along with the crumbling quiver. Later, I'd study them. Quickly, I returned to camp.

While the cattle crunched the old corn, we drank coffee out of tin cups. It was strong, delicious, and steaming hot. Never would I forget that coffee; no other tasted so fine. The cold, the intense situation, my fall into the kiva, the startling discovery of the arrowheads all heightened my senses to a degree of euphoria.

"Are you going to tell me now?" I asked the foreman my courage all geared up.

"Tell you what?" the foreman asked.

"What happened to them, your wife and son?" The expression of great sadness returned to his face and I realized that I had broken the spell that hung over the whole experience.

"I guess you've earned the right after all you've been through, Boy. Remember this as long as you live. Mistakes of extreme carelessness can never be corrected. We spend the rest of our lives being punished for them."

"But God wouldn't punish you," I began, but was quickly interrupted.

"God is God all by Himself. We humans are responsible. Great tragedies can't be blamed on the Almighty."

"Will you please tell me what happened?" I pleaded.

"Yes, I'll tell you, but once I finish, we must never speak of it again, not to anyone, do you hear me?"

"Yes sir."

"By chance I went to Kansas on a cattle drive with my herd. Those cattle were fat and healthy; they'd had a good spring, plenty to eat. I'd done trading before and knew the business. I was already rich off my cows. But this herd would make me richer. So I sold them. The buyer asked me to have dinner with his family. I'd always been a loner, but he was kind to me, so I agreed. Fate would have it that his daughter was home from school. When she came down the staircase, cows, money, food, I forgot everything. She was beautiful in a way no sunset could match nor any evening star. Her blue eyes, alabaster skin, delicate features, along with hair the color of sun burnished gold turned me speechless. She wasn't a girl who knew she was beautiful. I couldn't speak through the entire meal except to stammer and stutter and turn beet red from embarrassment. I made a real fool of myself.

"A year later I had to return on business. I'd put all of it behind me never expecting to see her again. Once again, fate would have it that I ran into her father at the bank. Once more, he asked me to dinner. Thinking since it was highly unlikely I'd have the same experience again, I accepted.

Who should open the door for us except that same young girl. She was a grown up young woman now. I made an exceptional fool of myself this time. She tried to make conversation, call me out by being polite, asking me questions about my ranch. But I had only one thing to say. I asked her to marry me."

"Right there at the dinner table?"

"Yes, right there at the dinner table."

"That's not the proper place," I said.

"Proper or not, I did it and the young lady didn't laugh or scold me or play the coquette. 'No,' she said so kindly, 'but, if you return in one year and still feel this way, I will marry you.' Her father was the one who laughed. His daughter was only seventeen."

"What did you do?" I asked.

"Went home, lost my courage. I figured she didn't mean it anyway. I spent a miserable year worrying. Then a letter came. She wrote that she'd behaved improperly and had no right to make such an offer, that I was off the hook if I wanted. No bad feelings, no lost hope or honor."

"What happened then?" I asked excitedly.

"A man doesn't get a second chance on his heart. She'd already won mine. I went to Kansas. We were married a month later. No sweeter, finer, more beautiful bride ever lived. This girl was smart, educated, a lady beyond imagination. We returned to my ranch and she told me that our child would be born in the fall. I was the happiest man alive."

Here the foreman paused and stood. "What were their names?" I asked quietly.

Standing over the fire, watching out of the shelter, he wore an unbearable pained expression like someone about to cry. He wiped his eyes. The snow stopped suddenly. I knew our time was running out. We'd have to return today.

"Her name was Jo Anna and our son's name was Armistice."

"Why on earth did you name him Armistice?"

"Funny you should ask that. It doesn't matter a hang now. Just before he was born, Jo Anna got homesick. She cried every day and wished for her Dad. She was afraid. We quarreled. I forbid her to travel in her condition. Later that night, she slipped into my room and told me the baby was coming. I went crazy trying to get dressed, find my boots, saddle my horse and go for the doctor. I knew the child was early and she was so young. She just laughed and said, "We'll call him Armistice."

"Him," I shouted.

"Him," she confirmed. It was a difficult birth. Twice she seemed to nearly perish. She wanted a priest. I'd almost forgotten that she was Catholic. I'd seen her pray her beads and she'd set up some altar in the spare room with the Blessed Virgin's picture. She gathered flowers and placed them there.

"Don't die, Jo Anna. Don't," I'd said loudly. She was so swollen and delirious. The doctor and his assistant told me to leave that the baby was about to be born."

The foreman paused. Melting snow dripped off the precipice. He put his hands to his face. I saw the toll this had taken on him. Exhaustion marked his features. Still he continued.

"Her recovery was long, but the boy thrived. We had a party for his first birthday. All the neighbors for twenty miles came. We even had fireworks. Jo Anna looked like the young girl I'd first met.

"Nearly a year later, the boys and I were rounding up cows. I had twenty-one steers penned. They broke loose and stampeded the rest. Two hundred wild cattle racing across the prairie are impossible to stop. A storm was approaching from the west. It began to thunder, lightning flashed. We tried to head them toward a canyon, thinking we'd capture them. Only about that time, a lone rider came traveling toward us. The cattle spooked, turned, running like demons toward the rider. It was too late. We all watched in shock as the cattle ran down the rider.

Once the dust cleared I rode to see who it was. The rain had started. It was Jo Anna and the boy. She was barely alive, but she smiled and whispered, 'I'm sorry.' I wiped the blood away from the corner of her mouth. She was gone. The boy lay beside her. I shot the poor horse. In numb grief, we held their funeral. The same people who'd come for the party, came for the funeral. At last she had the priest saying words over her beneath the picture of the Blessed Virgin she loved.

My brother took over running the ranch, having left his job and brought his family here. For years I was inconsolable. Then one night

Jo Anna appeared to me in a dream. She was so beautiful, her form incandescent.

'Don't grieve anymore,' she said softly in her well-remembered voice. 'I'm here, I'll wait for you.' She faded away and was gone.

"After that I began to do a hired hand's job. A little later, your dad promoted me to foreman."

"My Dad?" I asked breathless.

"Yes son, your dad is my brother."

Stunned, I ran to him and threw my arms around him. We both wept, him in grief, me in joy. Our foreman saw me off to college, saw me married, saw me hold my first son in my arms. He was the best friend I ever had. True to our vow we never spoke again of his great loss. Our foreman worked the ranch, tended his beloved cows. He knew every cow and calf by face, and the sound of their voice.

The arrowheads were carelessly tossed with my saddle bags in the barn. After the revelation at the snow bound cave, I never thought of them. Then one day years later, when we cleaned out the tack room, they fell from the weathered old saddle bag. Twenty-seven arrowheads lay on the floor. They were points of great beauty, probably new when lost, for they appeared pristine. When our foreman saw them, his first words were, "You must take them back. The spirits have been kind. You could have brought evil on this family. We must ride first thing in the morning and return the arrowheads."

He was old now, so I didn't object or argue. We saddled up at the first light and rode. When we reached the canyon he turned to me and said, "You saved my life, Boy. I'd drank for thirty years till the day we were stranded here. You made me tell it and it was all over at last."

"What about Jo Anna?" I queried.

"She was a saint. God took her young. He always takes the saints young. Those poor beasts, they didn't know. Only fear drove them that day."

We walked the canyon together, the ruins were more crumbled, a soft rose color. We found the kiva I'd fallen into. Then we went to the sight where I'd discovered the arrowheads. I placed them carefully. They shone like jewels for they were greatly polished. It was a ceremony, a ritual in strict accordance with the life our foreman had lived. We made a campfire and boiled coffee. He was an old, old man now, our foreman, eighty-six years. There were no tales to be told, no adventures to take, only two men sharing a campfire, a copper sunset, and coffee.

I can hear his words now, "In my heaven, all the angels will be cows because on earth I have loved them so dearly."

A month later, our foreman was suddenly stricken and gone. Our foreman was always my true north. I shall miss him the rest of my life.

7

THE FAWN

"Come see what I have on the back porch," Grandma said taking our hands leading us along. My brother and I were young children who admired Grandma more than anyone.

She opened the back screen door and there huddled on a make shift bed was the most magnificent creature we'd ever seen. A fawn, very tiny, with white spots and enormous brown eyes, lay folded on the pallet. It didn't move at all as it heard Grandma's voice. Grandma touched her fingers to the milk in her milk bucket and held out her hand. Instantly the fawn responded by licking the milk off Grandma's fingers. There was a hushed reverence over us because we'd never witnessed such a miracle.

Grandma told us that Grand Daddy had found the tiny fawn in the field while cutting the first spring hay crop. Its mother either had been too afraid and left it, or, simply not returned in time to fetch it before the hay machines roared across the field. Mother deer often leave their young while they go graze and forage, but once human hands touch the fawn, the mother will never accept it again. Grandma and the fawn bonded like mother and child. She raised her on cow's milk. As spring turned into summer, the fawn's legs grew long and her spots faded. The little creature loved and trusted Grandma above all else. She followed Grandma around like a puppy. Each evening when Grandma milked old, Susie, the cow, she'd put her hand in the milk bucket and hold it out to the fawn and let it lick the milk off her fingers. She gave the evening milk to the cats in the barn. The morning milk she saved and made butter. The cream she kept. We watched her many times strain the milk through a gauze cloth. She put it in a large glass container for us to drink later.

The fawn grew into a healthy, beautiful, graceful mahogany colored young animal. Timid around strangers, the young fawn hovered near Grandma's slim figure, certain of her protection. Her favorite treat besides milk was Grandma's roses. We became accustomed to the young deer grazing in Grandma's yard, nibbling at the roses,

In those days, deer were not so numerous in this part of Texas. It was rare to see them. Weeks would pass without sighting a single one, then we'd spot a group in the field. Our farm had vast acreage, and was thickly wooded, making it easy for deer to hide.

One late autumn day, we visited Grandma and became immediately aware of a great loss. Grandma's face was pale, and her eyes were red from crying. "I don't know where she went," Grandma said through her tears. "I came home from town and walked out to milk Susie like I always do when it dawned on me. I was alone. I ran everywhere and looked, but she's gone. I guess she grew up and the call of the wild was stronger than any love she felt for me. She has run away. I'll never see her again."

Many months passed and Grandma's sadness had eased a little, though she still looked for the fawn, when she went to milk Susie.

The deer had been gone a year, when one evening after Grandma finished milking the cow she turned and suddenly there stood a young doe. Grandma's heart beat wildly. Could it be her? Grandma dipped her fingers in the milk bucket and held out her hand to the deer. She gently licked the milk off, totally unafraid. Then she turned and gracefully walked down the hill. Grandma gasped. Waiting for the doe were two tiny fawns. "You brought your babies to show me," Grandma said. The deer looked for a long time at Grandma. The sun had set and it was nearly nightfall. In the twilight, the young doe walked away with her twins. Grandma never saw her again, but that memory stayed locked in her heart forever.

8

THE ILLUMINATOR

The wood line of trees, some ten to fifteen thousand, all heights and widths stood along the river bank in a haze of lilac and platinum. Overhead thousands, not hundreds, but thousands of crows and buzzards flew in groups toward the river. The buzzards glided gracefully; the crows flapped their wings while they cawed.

The sunset was coming fast, crimson and pure gold so stunning that there was sure to be a cold spell on the way. If only those fifteen mama cows and my old crippled bull hadn't gone across the river, I might have made it home before dark. There wouldn't even be a porch light to greet me now. Dark was only twenty minutes away.

Suddenly the wind shifted directly out of the north blowing a cold so fierce that it went straight through my denim jacket. Pulling it tighter around me, I turned my horse into a dark section of woods toward the river.

Cows lived according their never-ending hunger. They almost never stopped eating. That's what drove these across the river. Grass grew in abandoned pastures, knee high, green as spring. The cows weren't fools so off they went to their feast. They weren't going to be easy to bring home by one lone horseman.

When I came out of the woods, the sky was black with buzzards and crows cawing wildly, not a shaft of light coming through. I rode my horse down a steep incline along a deer trail and crossed the river. The cows didn't even glance in my direction.

Just then the first snow flake hit me in the face. A second and a third followed by a flurry. Now, I knew why all those birds were flying to the woods for cover. My fleet-footed horse was way ahead of me. He circled around the cows and headed them homeward. Cold sleety wind caused me to shiver, my teeth chattering uncontrollably. Biting one or two heifers on their rumps, my horse made fast work of the round-up. Still there was no sight of the bull. Back across the river, the cows raced ahead of my horse, white-tail deer startled and scattered. The cows ran to a broken section of fence, so I knew where it needed mending. I'd put these girls in the corral next to the barn so they wouldn't escape again. Tomorrow, I'd fix the fence.

My horse did all the work so it seemed as if I was simply along for the ride. The snow was falling fast and hard by the time I slammed the barn gate shut. I put my horse in the barn, unsaddled him, then rubbed him down and poured him some oats. Finally I threw some hay to the heifers and opened a gate to a covered lot so they'd be out of the snow. Then I remembered tomorrow was Christmas Eve.

The fire had burned down to embers in the parlor. Once I lit a lantern I saw what a miserable housekeeper I'd become. Dishes piled in the sink and the coffee pot on the stove reminded me that I hadn't eaten all day. Running a thousand acres of ranch wasn't easy for one man. All the hired help had moved on after my dad passed. Guess they figured by myself I'd never make a go of it bringing their pay checks to nothing. They went to search for something better so they believed.

My dear mother gone three years now, had kept the house spotless and something cooking on the stove day and night, even if it was just coffee brewing along with a pan of cinnamon cakes. Gradually the fire came to life after I added pine kindling, a log of pecan with one oak seasoned from last year. My brother rode off five years ago without a thought to any of us, breaking my mother's heart as well as dad's. They watched the door for him every evening till they died. The unutterable sorrow he gave them caused me so much bitterness that in my blackest moods I swore I'd never forgive him.

Still I held on, managing the ranch along with the funerals of my parents. Spring had brought the biggest calf crop I'd ever known. With the help of a few neighbor boys that summer, we drove the calves to market. I paid the boys, the taxes and the debts.

Scrambling some eggs for supper, I downed two cups of coffee chasing away the last bit of cold from my half frozen body. Tomorrow, I'd clean up the kitchen, sweep the floors, pull down the cobwebs, mend that fence, maybe even put up a Christmas tree to decorate with mother's beloved ornaments.

In my cold room in what used to be mother and dad's four poster mahogany bed, I straightened the quilts, crawled under those covers to get the scare of my life. My old cat, Sisse, came through a hole in the screen of an open window I'd forgotten to close. Her fur stood up for I'd spooked her too. We were both asleep almost before I blew out the lamp. My final thought was, tomorrow I'd fix the window.

Hours later a great knocking sounded on the main front door. Sisse screeched in terror, tearing through the window maybe never to return. Crawling out from the mountain of quilts, I scrambled to the seldom-used door. When I opened it, a sight that became indelible to my mind, greeted me.

A young woman not over twenty, covered in snow, so luminous as to be an apparition, stood before me, holding onto the hands of two small shivering children. I scratched my head in puzzlement, standing in my bright red union suit, when one of the children said, "Look, it's Santa Claus!" Unused to visitors, bitter of temperament, I stared into the snowy night wondering if this were real.

The young woman pulled back her hood from the cape she wore. "We lost our way in the storm. The horses bolted when our wagon wheel broke. We're nearly frozen, could we take shelter for a while till the storm ends?"

Continuing to stare, I saw that there was no chance of the storm ending soon, for already the snow was knee deep. More blew in waves of fine crystal across the lovely face of the girl. "Yes, come in. Where's my manners?" I said.

Once they entered the parlor, I added more wood to the coals, lit a lantern, dressed, all the while worrying what to do with such visitors.

By the lamp light I saw clearly the fine fair features of the young woman: lovely brown eyes, sharp brows above them, the color of her dark hair, pink lips revealing perfect white teeth. The only other woman I'd ever seen close up was my sister, Sarah, who died at age fourteen of pneumonia. My own dear mother's beauty was mature and serene. But this young woman's beauty was unique and mysterious, pure, like the Blessed Virgin Mary. There was an almost magical quality about her like the Christmas we were about to celebrate.

"Where exactly were you and your children going when your horses bolted?"

"Oh, I'm not married," said my young visitor as my mouth gaped at her. "These children are orphans, left to my care when my older sister and her husband died of fever last spring."

"Santa Claus," said the sweet-faced little girl who had warmed herself by the fire and shed her coat. "Are you going to get us a Christmas tree and toys?"

"He's not Santa, darling," the young woman began. "Oh, and by the way my name is…"

At that moment the little boy raced through the parlor in fast pursuit of Sisse. The young woman handed me the little girl, then ran to catch the boy. "Nathan, you stop chasing that cat right now," she said.

After giving the children some warm milk and crackers, I showed the young woman where they could sleep. When I went to offer them more quilts, they were all tucked away sleeping soundly in my bed. Sisse and I were left sitting by the fire wondering about our guests who had come upon us as suddenly as the winter storm.

In the hall closet were all of mother's things. I went and took down a dusty box. Mother's Christmas ornaments shined and sparkled like jewels in the long-stored box, keepsakes from childhood. Mother's family had been wealthy or my dad would never have owned our farm. Mother never returned home after I was born. As the years passed, the ornaments became especially cherished mementos.

I'd found a doll wrapped in paper and put away, belonging to my sister. Mother had stored a wooden pony and rider that was mine.

I carefully wrapped the toys in colored paper from a box I discovered in the closet, seldom if ever opened since Mother died. A special treasure I'd hesitated to wrap, but at last gave over to my better instincts, was for the young woman. I'd never forget for the rest of my life, her young pure face in the lantern light at my front door. At first light, I took off across the dazzling snow to give the little girl and little boy what they gone to sleep wishing for.

The perfect tree stood before me in the meadow. Quickly I cut it, tied it to my sleigh behind my horse and headed through the thick deep snow homeward.

When the children saw the tree bedecked with mother's ornaments, they squealed with delight. The parlor was warm and enchanted by the stately Christmas tree. Mother's ornaments, German, hand-made, of startling beauty caused the little girl to gasp in awe. Something in her expression made me stare. No, it couldn't be, not after all this time. Must be a trick of fatigue. Still, I wondered.

"Santa," the little girl said, "Where are the gifts?"

Though I'd wrapped them, the gifts were still in Mother's closet.

"Santa will bring the gifts tonight, darling." The young woman explained with a question mark in her eyes.

I nodded, wondering how I'd ever bring Christmas for these children. Mother had always done everything with such ease.

The young woman put out her hand, "I wanted to introduce myself. My name is.."

At that moment, the logs shifted, sparks flew and the little girl ran, jumping into my arms crying. "Santa Claus!"

"Tim," I said, putting out my free hand.

"Jennie," said the young woman laughing. "You already know Nathan." The boy bowed slightly, taking after Sisse who had tip-toed in to take a look at the resplendent Christmas tree.

"Why don't you tell me your name," I said to the little girl huddled in my arms.

"Millie," she answered promptly.

I gulped. Millie had been my mother's name. Carefully I placed the small girl on the floor, warmed by human presence. The house had been empty so long.

"Jennie, can you cook?" I asked.

"Oh, yes, very well. My parents sent me to the school of culinary arts. I was about to graduate when my sister became ill last spring. Afterwards, I stayed to take care of these children and settle affairs. We were traveling to my parents home when the storm caught us unexpectedly. Of course I'll cook breakfast." Jennie smiled.

"Nathan and I will go tend the cows I brought home yesterday evening." I explained while studying Millie's face.

When Nathan and I returned, the kitchen was warm, the dishes washed, coffee made and a stack of pancakes waited. "Hurry, Santa Claus," said Millie. "We're hungry."

I carried the bucket of milk that I'd brought from the barn. Our old cow, Georgia was foot to foot till I'd milked her.

As I sat down and started to take a bite, Millie grabbed my hand, "Prayers," she whispered. We all bowed our heads as little Millie said a blessing to put me to shame. My face, beet red and tears stinging my eyes, I looked at Jennie.

"We're Catholic," she announced. "These children learned early. Now it will stay with them all their lives.

Shy as he was, Nathan announced. "There's a baby calf in the barn with an old, old cow who might be his grandma."

We all laughed between bites of pancakes.

"No Nathan, Georgia is his mother. She is old, but she's always had healthy calves," I explained.

"He's real furry." Nathan added.

"To keep warm in this bitter cold," I told him. "I don't suppose you could ride to the river with me to find our old bull, could you Nathan?" I asked.

His eyes grew bright and hopeful as he looked at Jennie. "Could I? he begged.

"Of course," Jennie answered. "Millie and I will make sense of this kitchen."

At that moment Sisse came in and jumped right into Nathan's lap. We all laughed as I realized that God does work in mysterious ways, His wonders to behold.

Nathan was a timid boy, but once we reached the river and he saw the open sky, his timidness vanished. "Look, Tim, there's your old bull across the river. He's just lying there under the tree out of the snow."

"Well, we'll get him up with this sweet mash I brought along," I explained.

The snow was deep, but we crossed the river carefully. I got off my horse, went to my old bull holding the sweet mash close enough for him to smell. He took a whiff, stood up and was ready to follow us anywhere.

"Look, Tim, he's decorated for Christmas," Nathan laughed, pointing to my bull's curly forehead. Strands of red berries and mistletoe tangled with his curls. "He's really big," Nathan observed, looking at the giant Black Angus bull that I called, Baby.

"Let's take him home, Nathan. You rattle that bucket of sweet mash and he'll tag along."

Nathan's smile warmed my heart more than anything in recent time. It was tough going through the deep snow. Baby had an old injury to his hip. Arthritis had claimed it causing him to limp. The sky was a clear azure blue, the clearest I ever remembered. The river was a deep emerald against the snow banks. Nathan and I rode in silence. Baby, the bull, followed slowly for the hope of a breakfast of sweet mash.

"Is he a pet, Tim?"

"Who, Nathan?"

"Your bull."

"Guess you could call him a pet. I've known him all his life since he was born. I nursed him through a storm of sickness when the other bulls fought him, broke his shoulder and injured his hip."

"What did you do?" asked Nathan.

"Rounded up all those trouble-makers and sold them. Then I brought Baby to the barn, nursed his wounds, gave him lots of fresh hay, let him lay up and heal. That's when he got fond of sweet mash. Come spring, I turned him out to graze, but he didn't want to go. He was afraid those other bulls were waiting to attack him again. He was so vulnerable as a young calf, orphaned after his mother died."

"Like me?" Nathan asked.

"You have Jennie."

"No, she's not my mother. Mama was blonde and sweet and read stories to Millie and me. When she died I wanted to go with her wherever it is they go, but Jennie said I had to stay behind."

"Heaven is where they go, Nathan. Heaven is where we finish up after this life on earth is over. It's the promise God gave us. But where was your dad?"

"Oh he was hardly ever around until Mama got real sick. Then he came back home, took sick too. Him and Mama died together. Millie and I hardly knew him. How do you know all these things, Tim?"

"I'm older, Nathan, way down life's road. You're just starting down that road. God has some marvelous plan for your life, Nathan. Just watch it unfold. I don't mean that you'll never have anything bad happen because you will. I don't mean you won't have bad days because you will. Through it all, you'll be able to see God's hand in your life."

"Jennie never told us any of this." Nathan admitted.

"That's because she was too busy taking care of you and Millie. Jennie is a good, fine girl, not much more than a child herself," I impressed.

"She is a real good cook," Nathan said with certainty.

"We're about to find out as soon as we get Baby bedded down."

Nathan was right. My neighbor had brought a Christmas turkey. Jennie had stuffed it with rice and baked it, made gravy, some dried vegetables and bread, golden brown. The table was set with mother's china, silver and linen.

"Should I put on a dinner jacket?" I asked.

Blushing deeply, Jennie smiled and answered "Of course not. Let's eat the food while it's hot."

I took my place at the head of the table, savoring the aromas. "I'm impressed, Jennie. It's been a long while since I sat down to an elegant meal," I complimented the young woman who'd turned up on my door step a mere twenty-four hours ago.

"My old cow, Rebecca, had a calf last night." I said to Jennie as if I'd known her, as if she was a relative, as if she was my wife, "Now we'll have milk and cream."

"And butter," Jennie added smiling.

"Once the snow is gone, we can go hunt your horses. Someone is bound to have found them by now."

We all sat down at the table. Millie put her hands together and bowed her head.

I looked across the table at Jennie. "Prayers," she smiled.

I though of all the meals I'd eaten standing in the kitchen alone. Nathan had his head bowed too. My eyes questioned Jennie.

"They're waiting for you to give thanks before everything gets cold." Jennie explained. My eyes filled with tears. What had I to give thanks for until now? All I could utter was, "Lord, we thank you for everything. Amen"

Jennie, Nathan and Millie repeated. "Amen."

Christmas morning dawned cold and bleak. I knew it would be some time before my guests could leave. I'd carefully placed the three gifts under the shining tree. I lay on my mother's parlor sofa, weary in every bone. Suddenly the door burst open. The children ran in excitedly. They headed straight for the tree. I noticed the odd expression in Jennie's eyes.

"Here," I said handing a large amateur-wrapped gift to Nathan.

"Thanks," he said and began tearing off the paper.

Millie stood quietly waiting to accept her gift. Little astonished sounds came from her as I handed the giant package to her. "Thank you, Santa Claus," she said.

Lastly, I gave Jennie her gift. She blushed deeply, glancing away. "We have nothing to give you," she said.

"Oh, you've given me plenty, the chance to be a host again, the chance to eat good food, the chance to think of someone other than myself, rare gifts," I assured her.

"Like the wise men in the story," Nathan suggested. He stood holding the wooden horse and rider.

Millie held the doll as if it were alive.

"Open yours," I hastened Jennie.

Carefully, she removed the paper, gently tugging the white ribbon loose.

She opened the small velvet box. An expression of complete awe came across her face.

Tears stood in her eyes. "Oh, Nathan, Millie, look," she said.

"It is like the wise men," Nathan confirmed.

A small, intricate cross of tiny diamonds was a gift from my dad to Mother many years ago. I never saw her wear it, but she took if from the velvet box and studied it
several times a year as if to reaffirm her faith.

"Thank you." Jennie expressed shyly.

"Perhaps, you'll allow me to fix the clasp for you." I said and went to stand behind her. When she lifted her brown hair, I saw how white and flawless her neck was .

A week passed, then two. A distant neighbor rode over to tell me that he'd found
two horses still harnessed. I asked him to keep them for a bit.

The New Year had begun with me holding onto the fragile gifts I'd received at Christmas. They were three human gifts, who had become as dear to me as my own family: Jennie, Nathan and Millie. I dreaded approaching Jennie about the horses. It would mean they'd be leaving soon.

The weather had turned almost balmy. The snow was completely gone. I stood on the back porch of the old Victorian house. The sky had produced a good crop of stars. Jennie came outside to join me, her shyness apparent still.

"Did you get Nathan and Millie settled for the night?" I queried.

"Yes, but only after two long stories," Jennie admitted. Again she cast a wistful look.

I turned to her, "What is it Jennie? What do you want to say?"

She blushed again. "I'm not sure. There's been something troubling me since the moment I first saw you."

"What?"

"I'm probably wrong."

"Tell me and let's see if you're wrong."

"When I first saw you," Jennie began. "The moment you opened the door in the snow..." She stopped. "No I'm probably wrong."

"Go ahead, Jennie. We know each other well enough to reveal a confidence."

"When I first saw you, I was stunned. You looked enough like my sister's husband to pass for his twin, older but nearly identical. Later I thought it was a trick of the light."

"What did the children think?"

"That you were kind, considerate, and wonderful. But they barely knew their father. And once someone dies, memory usually fades quickly, especially in children."

At that moment, Millie came onto the porch, holding her doll, wearing one of my sister Sarah's, old night gowns that Mother had saved.

"You'll catch cold, Millie," Jennie scolded.

"Here, let me," I offered, gathering Millie in my arms to carry her back to bed.

As I tucked her under the quilts, she called softly, "Santa Claus."

"It's getting late," Jennie said. I shouldn't leave Millie again. Sometimes she still has nightmares. She misses her mother."

Since New Year's Eve, I'd been sleeping in the guest room, but after Jennie's declaration, I went to rest on the sofa in the parlor. My guests were nearing the end of their visit. We'd recovered their wagon. My distant neighbor brought their horses back.

Neither Jennie nor I had discussed our near discovery. We didn't dare.

Jennie was an intelligent girl. By the soft gasp that escaped her lips and her hand covering her mouth immediately afterwards, I think she knew nearly as well as I what we had happened upon. Sometimes truth is frightening and doesn't bear facing. Jennie and I were both afraid of what the truth would mean in our lives.

The trouble was that I had fallen in love with my new found family of two sweet-faced children and a girl so beautiful that it took my breath away just to look at her. For a man nearly thirty-eight years old, change was an important decision.

After an extremely hard day of fence building, rounding up strays and patching the barn where two young fighting bulls had crashed into the east side, exhaustion took me. I fell into bed like the old days before my guests came. Out like a light. Sometime later, a light was shining in my face, a lantern light. Behind it stood Nathan.

"Tim, there's an old cow at the barn trying to have a calf."

"How do you know that, Nathan?" I asked, rubbing the sleep from my eyes.

"Feet."

"Feet?"

"There's feet coming out of the back of her."

"Oh no, it's old Kate," I said, thinking how she'd lost her last two calves.

Nathan was a born natural. He found the rope, the calf-puller, got hot water, then he held the lantern while I made a clumsy attempt to deliver the calf. Hours later, old Kate delivered a fine bull calf.

Nathan smiled in the dim light and said "Ain't that the beautifulest sight you ever saw, Tim?"

"Isn't it?" I agreed as the tiny calf nursed.

"I'm a right fair farm hand, Tim. You could keep me when Jennie leaves with Millie. I'd help you out a bunch."

"You think so, Nathan?"

"Yep. This place feels like home."

For a man who seldom cried, I was sure having a problem lately.

"Put some fresh hay down for them. They'll want to rest now, Nathan."

"Me too," he said.

"Me too," I added as we walked home.

Their wagon repaired, their harnesses mended, their bags almost packed, my guests were in the final days of their visit. I'd promised Nathan a short trip to an old Indian camp ground up river. When I'd shown him the arrowheads I'd found there, he was adamant. "It may be my last chance, Tim," he insisted.

We saddled our horses and rose away before sun-up with Jennie waving goodbye at the back gate, after handing us a packed lunch. When I'd told her of our plans the day before, she shrugged and said, "Go. Millie and I will be fine."

The woods were alive with wildlife. Birds scattered upon our approach. Nathan whispered, "Tim, what's that?" pointing toward the river.

"Bob cat," I whispered back.

Nathan's eyes widened noticeably.

The morning was brisk, not bitter cold as in the previous weeks of endless snow and ice. A herd of white-tail deer ran from cover to the open, pausing to glance back at us before charging down the steep canyon slope to the green sparkle of river. Our horses spooked momentarily. A giant buck deer with a thick tangle of horns like old rose canes gazed steadily at us before dashing down a deep, gorged-out path.

We rode down a meandering cow trail, the quiet like the inside of a cave. Suddenly, an owl streaked out from the woods startling Nathan's horse. Both tumbled, falling straight down the river bank. I heard the sound of my own voice screaming, "Nathan!" What a fool I'd been to put a child on a horse.

In silence, I prayed. Leaving my horse tied some distance away, I went to stare down the river bank. Nathan lay sprawled at the water's edge, the horse standing over him unhurt. Making my way carefully down the deer trail, I finally reached Nathan. Blood ran from his mouth and he moaned.

"Nathan," I said. "Nathan, can you hear me?"

Slowly, his eyes opened. He smiled. "Tim, you never told me this could happen. I bit my tongue when I fell. I'm all right, Tim. Nothing broken, I'm just shook up."

I gathered him in my arms so swiftly that he cried out. Tears stung my eyes. That's when I saw the saw the unmistakable point of an Indian arrowhead sticking out of the river bank. Helping Nathan to his feet, I said, "Look!"

"Tim," he said excitedly, "Is it what I think it is?"

We both dug into the bank of the river, resulting in another crash. Dirt and grit rained down on us. We looked in disbelief.

The skeleton of a woman and a child lay in a cave-like enclave. The larger skeleton was certainly that of a woman because her arms held the smaller skeleton, a child. We stood mystified. How many decades had their tomb remained untouched?

Finally, Nathan spoke, "What should we do, Tim?"

"I'm not sure, Nathan. But now we have two problems. How do we get your horse back up this steep bank? And what do we do with these two people we've discovered?"

Nathan rushed forward, "Look Tim, the baby has a necklace. It must have been a girl."

Sure enough, bits of pearl mussel shell lay in a circle around the tiny neck. The string that held them long ago disintegrated. There was another surprise. The child clutched a doll made of stone, the face clearly carved into the sandstone.

"Wonder how they died?" Nathan asked softly.
"That, we'll never know, but death followed these people everywhere they went. They lived in a perilous time, Nathan."

Around the skeletons lay a circle of pristine arrowheads, some large, some small, as if they were an offering.

"We can't take them, can we, Tim?" Nathan asked.

"I think not," I began, "There's some who would call it superstition or religion. We'll leave them as we found them undisturbed. We'll put the dirt back, cover them."

"What about the arrowhead that fell out from the bank?" Nathan asked.

Morals, rules, lessons, and discipline were hard enough to teach a child. I hesitated to answer.

"Tim?" Nathan asked again.

"Well, Nathan, let's rebury them and we'll think on it," I told him.

We used some large shells found near the water's edge to put the dirt back into the cave opening. The woman must have been very young. Her teeth were excellent, straight, even, all intact. She must have been loved as indicated by the way she and the child were buried. Her people must have grieved over their loss.

"Should we pray, Tim?" Nathan said.

"You pray. You pray for them, Nathan."

Without a thought, the small boy dropped to his knees. So touched was I that I knelt down too. An answer to all my wondering came as he began the Lord's Prayer. Jennie had done well. She had planted a seed and it has blossomed in this child.

I allowed Nathan to take the arrowhead we'd discovered. A few stone beads lay nearby. Since there was no way to determine where they belonged for certain, I let him take those as well, evidence of our discovery. Nathan carefully wrapped the uniquely beautiful arrowhead and the tiny beads in his handkerchief.

It began to rain heavily, down pour after down pour. We carefully walked up river and found another crossing that wasn't so steep. Nathan surprised me by leading his horse straight up the river bank. Night was coming fast. We hunched over our horses, pulled our collars up tight and our hats down low, but the rain drenched us. It was slow going in the blinding rain.

"I know an old hunter's cabin not far," I called to Nathan. "We'll try and make that."

Once, I feared we'd lost our way until in the dim twilight I saw the outline of the cabin. We put our horses in the semi-collapsed shed near the cabin. Inside we fell exhausted on the earthen floor, unaware of our surroundings. The dark night soon covered us.

Nathan and I never heard the rain stop. Exhausted as we were from our long journey, Nathan's fall, and the discovery of the sacred tomb, we slept.

Hours later, the cabin door burst open with a gray-streaked sky pouring over us. At that moment I came fully awake. A dripping wet Jennie tugging Millie behind her struggled toward us. The sensation of holding Jennie in my arms for the first time was a moment of rare grandeur. The scent of her damp clothes, the infinitesimal touch of her smooth face against mine, and her soft whimpering voice still come to me on the quietest nights.

Millie said, "Oh, Santa Claus, we found you."

Did Jennie and I marry? Our wedding was the most talked about for years, a forever marriage. My surprised neighbors had assumed that I would always remain a lonely old bachelor.

The priest couldn't stop smiling as he said, "Dearly beloved, we are gathered here in the presence of God to witness and bless the joining together of this man and this woman in Holy Matrimony."

Did Jennie and I ever tell Nathan and Millie about their father, my brother? We did not. There was no time for sadness. Jennie became their mother and I their father, raising them as our own children.

Millie went away to school, returned a teacher, just in time to replace our retiring headmistress of our one room school. The children adored Millie. To this day she still calls me, Santa Claus.

Our Nathan manages this farm now with his two young sons. Needless to say, it has greatly prospered.

And Jennie. The only betrayal of her age are a few strands of silver hair and just a hint less gold in her skin. To me, Jennie will always be bedazzling.

On days when I can climb on my horse, I ride out to scan the farthest horizon. I recall with reverence the long ago Christmas when the hand of the Eternal One guided three strangers through a blizzard to my front door.

Readers Guide and Discussion Questions

I. The Well

Why do you think Totto believed Mr. Arlo Winchester Lowrey concerning the legend of the lost well? What do you think Totto learned from his adventure with Mr. Lowrey?

2. The Hundred Year Old Cow

Do you think cows feel pain the same as humans? Do you believe that cows feel affection toward humans? Do you think cows are afraid of death?

3. The Cowboy

What was the reason the cowboy volunteered to watch the cow herd alone? Was his reasoning off because of his broken romance? Could his untimely death have been avoided?

4. Stuck

Is humor necessary to keep a healthy mental attitude? Was Belinda a stepping stone to healing the grief? Do you believe Belinda had superior intelligence?

5. Ode To A Wedding

Did you know that very old cows could still give birth to healthy calves? Was Bessie Milsap an example of a crusader for women's rights? Would the marriage with Grisham Graham Ingleholt work out? Were both Bessie and Grisham strong personalities or was Grisham a weakling? Do you think the old cow brought Bessie and Grisham together?

6. Mystery At Adobe Canyon

Why was Boy never told that the foreman was his uncle? Was the foreman a secret drinker? Did Boy already love the foreman before their adventure or, was he merely curious about him? Was their interaction the beginning of the foreman's healing? Why did the foreman have such strong principles yet he drank? Why was Boy so influenced by the foreman?

7. The Fawn

Do some people become too attached to animals/pets? Do animals have strong attachments to humans? Why did Grandma love the fawn so strongly? Why did the fawn never return after her appearance with her twins?

8. The Illuminator

Was Tim content running a ranch and living alone? Did Christmas bring extra meaning to Tim's sudden arrival of guests? Did the possibility of being related draw Tim closer to Millie and Nathan? Did the adventure Tim and Nathan have cause Tim to realize what he had found in his relationship with Jennie, Millie and Nathan? Were romance and relationships more important to people a generation ago?

Was life better a century ago? Were people of higher morals and more heroic?